TAMING ANXIETY AND ANGER:

Life Skills Every Teen Needs to Take Control

While every precaution has been taken in the preparation of this book, the publisher assumes no responsibility for errors or omissions, or for damages resulting from the use of the information contained herein.

TAMING ANXIETY AND ANGER

First edition. September 22, 2024.

Copyright © 2024 Darlington Appiah.

ISBN: 979-8227191373

Written by Darlington Appiah.

I DEDICATE THIS BOOK TO THE ALMIGHTY GOD TO
HELP ALL PEOPLE READING THIS BOOK TO BE ABLE TO
TAME ANXIETY AND ANGER

CHAPTER 1

Understanding Anxiety: A Comprehensive Guide

Anxiety is a pervasive condition that affects millions of people worldwide, including a significant number of teenagers. It can manifest in various forms and impact numerous aspects of daily life. To address anxiety effectively, it's essential to understand what it is, how it feels, and recognize the signs and symptoms that accompany it. This article will delve deeply into these aspects to provide a thorough understanding of anxiety, especially for those experiencing it.

What Is Anxiety?

Anxiety is a state of intense apprehension or worry about future events or situations. It is a natural response to stress and can serve as a protective mechanism when facing real threats. However, when anxiety becomes excessive, persistent, or irrational, it can hinder daily functioning and overall quality of life. For teens, who are navigating a period of significant change and stress, anxiety can be particularly challenging.

Anxiety disorders are characterized by chronic and excessive worry or fear that is difficult to control and often interferes with daily activities. There are several types of anxiety disorders, including Generalized Anxiety Disorder (GAD), Social Anxiety Disorder, Panic Disorder, and Specific Phobias.

Symptoms and Signs of Anxiety

Emotional Symptoms

1. Persistent Worry: One of the hallmark signs of anxiety is persistent, often irrational worry about everyday situations or future events. This worry can be about anything from academic performance to social interactions and personal safety. The anxiety often feels disproportionate to the actual threat or challenge.

2. Irritability: Anxiety can make individuals more irritable and easily agitated. Small issues or inconveniences that might not usually cause stress can lead to heightened frustration or anger.

3. Feeling Overwhelmed: Teens with anxiety may feel overwhelmed by their responsibilities and commitments. This can manifest as difficulty concentrating, procrastination, or a general sense of being unable to manage their tasks effectively.

Cognitive Symptoms

1. Racing Thoughts: Anxiety often leads to racing thoughts, where the mind constantly shifts between different worries and concerns. This mental chaos can make it challenging to focus on one task at a time and can contribute to feelings of being mentally drained.

2. Difficulty Concentrating: The intrusive nature of anxious thoughts can impair concentration, making it difficult for teens to focus on their studies, conversations, or other activities. This can negatively affect academic performance and social interactions.

3. Fear of the Worst-Case Scenario: Those with anxiety may have a tendency to imagine the worst possible outcomes in any given situation. This fear of what might go wrong can be paralyzing and lead to avoidance behaviors.

Physical Symptoms

1. Heart Palpitations: Anxiety can cause the heart to beat rapidly or irregularly. This sensation, known as palpitations, can be distressing and may exacerbate feelings of anxiety.

2. Sweating: Excessive sweating, particularly in situations that trigger anxiety, is a common physical response. This can occur even in the absence of physical exertion or heat.

3. Shaking or Trembling: Anxiety often manifests physically through shaking or trembling, which can be particularly noticeable in the hands or legs. This physical reaction can be a source of embarrassment and self-consciousness.

4. Muscle Tension: Chronic anxiety often leads to muscle tension, especially in areas such as the neck, shoulders, and jaw. This tension can cause discomfort and contribute to physical pain or headaches.

5. Nausea: Anxiety can also affect the gastrointestinal system, leading to feelings of nausea or stomach discomfort. This can impact appetite and eating habits, further contributing to stress.

Behavioral Symptoms

1. Avoidance: To escape anxiety-inducing situations, individuals might engage in avoidance behaviors. For example, a teen may avoid social gatherings or skip classes to evade the stress associated with these activities.

2. Restlessness: Anxiety often leads to a sense of restlessness, where individuals find it hard to sit still or relax. This restlessness can manifest as fidgeting, pacing, or an inability to settle down.

3. Procrastination: Due to overwhelming feelings of anxiety, individuals might procrastinate on tasks or responsibilities. This delay can further increase anxiety as deadlines approach or tasks pile up.

HOW ANXIETY FEELS PHYSICALLY AND EMOTIONALLY

Emotional Experience

Anxiety can feel like an emotional storm, characterized by an intense, often irrational, sense of dread or apprehension. It can be a persistent feeling of being on edge, accompanied by a pervasive sense of worry or fear. For many, anxiety feels like a heavy weight on their chest, a constant companion that interferes with their ability to enjoy life or engage in daily activities.

Emotionally, anxiety can create a rollercoaster of feelings. One moment, there might be a sense of calm, while the next, overwhelming worry takes over. This unpredictability can make it challenging to manage emotions and maintain a stable mood.

Physical Experience

Physically, anxiety can feel like a constant state of alertness or tension. The body's fight-or-flight response, which is typically triggered in dangerous situations, can become activated even in non-threatening scenarios. This response can cause various physical symptoms, including:

1. Increased Heart Rate: The sensation of a racing heart can be alarming and is a common physical symptom of anxiety. It often feels like the heart is pounding or fluttering, which can be distressing.

2. Shortness of Breath: Anxiety can cause a feeling of not getting enough air, leading to shortness of breath or a sensation of breathlessness. This can make it difficult to breathe deeply and comfortably.

3. Sweating: Excessive sweating, especially in situations where anxiety is high, can be uncomfortable and noticeable. This physical reaction is often accompanied by feelings of embarrassment or self-consciousness.

4. Muscle Tension: The body may feel tense and stiff, particularly in areas like the shoulders, neck, and jaw. This tension can lead to discomfort and contribute to headaches or other physical ailments.

5. Gastrointestinal Issues: Anxiety can affect the digestive system, leading to symptoms such as nausea, stomach cramps, or changes in appetite. These physical symptoms can further contribute to feelings of unease.

COPING WITH ANXIETY

Understanding the nature of anxiety is the first step toward managing it effectively. Here are some strategies that can help in coping with anxiety:

1. Practice Relaxation Techniques: Techniques such as deep breathing, progressive muscle relaxation, and mindfulness can help calm the mind and reduce physical symptoms of anxiety.

2. Challenge Negative Thoughts: Cognitive Behavioral Therapy (CBT) techniques can help individuals recognize and challenge irrational thoughts, replacing them with more balanced perspectives.

3. Engage in Physical Activity: Regular exercise can help reduce anxiety by releasing endorphins, which are natural mood lifters.

4. Seek Support: Talking to a trusted friend, family member, or mental health professional can provide relief and guidance in managing anxiety.

5. Establish a Routine: Maintaining a structured daily routine can help create a sense of stability and control, reducing anxiety levels.

6. Limit Caffeine and Sugar: Reducing the intake of stimulants like caffeine and sugar can help minimize anxiety symptoms, as these substances can exacerbate feelings of nervousness.

7. Practice Self-Care: Prioritizing self-care activities, such as getting enough sleep, eating a balanced diet, and engaging in hobbies, can contribute to overall well-being and reduce anxiety.

Anxiety is a complex and multifaceted condition that can have a profound impact on various aspects of life. By understanding its symptoms, physical and emotional experiences, and effective coping strategies, individuals can take proactive steps to manage their anxiety and improve their quality of life. If anxiety becomes overwhelming or persistent, seeking professional help is crucial in finding tailored support and treatment options. Remember, you're not alone in facing anxiety, and there are resources and strategies available to help navigate this challenging experience.

CHAPTER 2

Understanding Anger: A Comprehensive Guide

Anger is a fundamental human emotion experienced by everyone at various points in their lives. While anger is a natural response to perceived threats or injustices, it becomes problematic when it is intense, frequent, or mismanaged. For teens, navigating anger can be particularly challenging due to the numerous changes and pressures they face. This article provides an in-depth exploration of what anger is, common triggers, and how it affects individuals, with a focus on helping teens understand and manage their emotions more effectively.

What Is Anger?

Anger is a powerful emotion characterized by feelings of hostility, frustration, or irritation in response to perceived provocation or injustice. It is an evolutionary response that can serve as a defense mechanism, preparing individuals to confront or escape threats. While anger can be a healthy and necessary emotion, its expression and management are crucial for maintaining well-being and healthy relationships.

Types of Anger

1. Passive Anger: This form of anger is not openly expressed but is instead internalized. Individuals experiencing passive anger might suppress their feelings or exhibit passive-aggressive behaviors. This type of anger can lead to unresolved issues and internal stress.

2. Aggressive Anger: Aggressive anger involves outward expression, often through verbal or physical confrontations. It can be destructive and harmful, leading to conflicts and damaged relationships.

3. Assertive Anger: Assertive anger is expressed in a constructive manner. Individuals communicate their feelings clearly and respectfully without

aggression. This type of anger can lead to positive outcomes and problem resolution.

COMMON TRIGGERS OF ANGER

1. Frustration with Injustice or Unfairness

- Academic Pressures: Teens often face intense academic pressures, such as demanding coursework, high expectations, and extracurricular commitments. Feelings of unfair treatment by teachers or a perception of inequitable grading can trigger anger.

- Social Injustice: Witnessing or experiencing social injustice, such as bullying or discrimination, can provoke anger. Teens may feel frustrated when they perceive that they or others are being treated unfairly.

2. Interpersonal Conflicts

- Family Dynamics: Conflicts with family members, such as disagreements with parents or siblings, can be a significant source of anger. Issues such as lack of understanding or differing values can exacerbate these conflicts.

- Friendship Problems: Disagreements or betrayals among friends can lead to intense feelings of anger. Issues such as gossip, exclusion, or broken trust are common triggers in teen relationships.

3. Personal Frustrations

- Unmet Expectations: When personal goals or expectations are not met, teens may experience anger. This can include frustration over academic performance, social achievements, or personal aspirations.

- Perceived Lack of Control: Situations where teens feel powerless or unable to influence outcomes can lead to anger. This can include feeling controlled by external factors or experiencing restrictions on personal freedom.

4. External Stressors

- Life Changes: Major life changes, such as moving to a new school or dealing with family changes, can trigger anger. The stress and uncertainty associated with these changes can lead to emotional outbursts.

- Environmental Factors: Environmental stressors, such as noise, overcrowding, or chaotic surroundings, can contribute to feelings of irritation and anger.

5. Hormonal and Developmental Changes

- Puberty: Hormonal changes during puberty can impact mood and emotional regulation. Teens may experience increased sensitivity and heightened emotional responses, including anger.

- Identity Development: As teens explore their identity and seek independence, they may experience frustration and anger related to their evolving self-concept and autonomy.

HOW ANGER AFFECTS YOU

Emotional Impact

1. Emotional Instability: Anger can lead to fluctuations in mood, contributing to emotional instability. This can result in feelings of irritability, frustration, and heightened sensitivity.

2. Decreased Self-Esteem: Persistent anger can affect self-esteem, leading individuals to feel inadequate or incapable of managing their emotions. This can result in self-blame and reduced confidence.

3. Strained Relationships: Uncontrolled anger can strain relationships with family, friends, and peers. Frequent outbursts or aggressive behavior can lead to misunderstandings, conflicts, and diminished trust.

Cognitive Impact

1. Impaired Judgment: Anger can impair cognitive functioning, leading to poor decision-making and impaired judgment. When angry, individuals may act impulsively without considering the consequences of their actions.

2. Ruminative Thinking: Anger often leads to ruminative thinking, where individuals repeatedly focus on the source of their anger. This can perpetuate feelings of frustration and prevent constructive problem-solving.

3. Difficulty Concentrating: Anger can impact concentration and attention, making it challenging to focus on tasks or responsibilities. This can affect academic performance and daily functioning.

Physical Impact

1. Increased Stress Levels: Anger triggers the body's stress response, leading to increased levels of cortisol and adrenaline. This can result in physical symptoms such as increased heart rate, muscle tension, and elevated blood pressure.

2. Physical Health Issues: Chronic anger can contribute to various health issues, including headaches, digestive problems, and cardiovascular conditions. The ongoing stress associated with anger can negatively impact overall health.

3. Sleep Disturbances: Persistent anger can lead to sleep disturbances, including difficulty falling asleep or staying asleep. This can further exacerbate emotional and physical health problems.

Behavioral Impact

1. Destructive Behavior: Uncontrolled anger can lead to destructive behaviors, including verbal aggression, physical confrontations, or property damage. These behaviors can have serious consequences for relationships and personal well-being.

2. AVOIDANCE OR WITHDRAWAL: Some individuals may respond to anger by avoiding or withdrawing from situations or people. This can lead to isolation and a lack of resolution for underlying issues.

3. Impulsive Actions: Anger can lead to impulsive actions, where individuals act without considering the consequences. This can result in regretful decisions and strained relationships.

Managing and Transforming Anger

1. Recognize and Acknowledge Anger

- Identifying Triggers: Understanding what triggers your anger is the first step in managing it effectively. Keeping a journal of your anger experiences can help you identify patterns and specific triggers.

- Acknowledging Your Feelings: Accepting that anger is a natural emotion is crucial for managing it. Recognize that feeling angry is valid, but how you choose to express and handle it is within your control.

---

2. PRACTICE HEALTHY Expression

- Use Assertive Communication: Communicate your feelings clearly and respectfully. Avoid using aggressive or accusatory language, and focus on expressing how the situation affects you and what you need.

- Engage in Physical Activity: Physical exercise can be an effective outlet for anger. Activities such as running, swimming, or yoga can help release pent-up energy and reduce stress.

3. Employ Relaxation Techniques

- Deep Breathing: Practice deep breathing exercises to calm your body and mind. Deep, slow breaths can help reduce physiological arousal associated with anger.

- Progressive Muscle Relaxation: Use progressive muscle relaxation techniques to release physical tension. Tense and relax different muscle groups to promote relaxation and reduce anger.

4. Develop Problem-Solving Skills

- Focus on Solutions: Shift your focus from the problem to potential solutions. Identify practical steps you can take to address the issues causing your anger and work towards resolving them.

- Set Realistic Goals: Establish achievable goals for managing and transforming your anger. Break down larger goals into smaller, manageable steps to track your progress.

5. Seek Support

- Talk to a Trusted Person: Share your feelings with a trusted friend, family member, or counselor. Talking about your anger can provide relief and offer new perspectives on the situation.

- Professional Help: If anger becomes overwhelming or unmanageable, consider seeking help from a mental health professional. Therapy can provide valuable tools and strategies for managing anger effectively.

---

6. BUILD EMOTIONAL Resilience

- Practice Self-Care: Prioritize self-care activities that promote emotional well-being. Engage in hobbies, relaxation techniques, and activities that bring you joy and fulfillment.

- Cultivate Mindfulness: Practice mindfulness to increase awareness of your emotions and reactions. Mindfulness techniques can help you stay grounded and manage anger more effectively.

7. Develop Positive Coping Strategies

- Creative Outlets: Use creative outlets such as art, music, or writing to express and process your emotions. Creative activities can provide a constructive way to channel anger and promote emotional healing.

- Engage in Relaxation Activities: Incorporate relaxation activities into your routine, such as reading, taking baths, or spending time in nature. These activities can help reduce stress and improve overall well-being.

---

8. FOSTER POSITIVE Relationships

- Build Strong Connections: Strengthen relationships with supportive and understanding individuals. Surrounding yourself with positive influences can help you manage anger and navigate challenges more effectively.

- Practice Empathy: Develop empathy for others to improve communication and reduce conflicts. Understanding different perspectives can help you respond to situations with greater compassion and patience.

9. Address Underlying Issues

- Explore Root Causes: Examine underlying issues contributing to your anger. Addressing root causes, such as unresolved conflicts or unmet needs, can help reduce the intensity and frequency of anger.

- Work on Personal Growth: Engage in personal growth activities, such as self-reflection and goal setting, to address underlying emotional issues and enhance emotional resilience.

Understanding anger, its triggers, and its effects is essential for managing this powerful emotion effectively. By recognizing the sources of your anger, practicing healthy expression, and developing coping strategies, you can navigate your emotions in a constructive manner. Remember, anger

CHAPTER 3

The Connection Between Anxiety and Anger: A Deep Dive

Anxiety and anger are two powerful emotions that can significantly impact a person's life, particularly during adolescence—a time marked by profound emotional and psychological changes. While these emotions may appear distinct at first glance, they are intricately connected and often interact in complex ways. Understanding the relationship between anxiety and anger is crucial for effective emotional management and overall well-being. This article explores how anxiety and anger interact, recognizing overlaps in their symptoms, and provides strategies for managing these intertwined emotions.

How Anxiety and Anger Interact

1. Emotional Overlap

Anxiety and anger both involve heightened emotional responses, but they manifest differently. Anxiety is characterized by excessive worry and fear about future events or situations, while anger typically arises from perceived threats or injustices. Despite these differences, there is significant emotional overlap between the two.

- Heightened Arousal: Both anxiety and anger involve increased arousal and activation of the body's stress response system. When a person experiences anxiety, their body may enter a state of heightened alertness, similar to how it reacts to anger. This physiological response includes increased heart rate, rapid breathing, and muscle tension, which can contribute to both emotions.

- Fear and Threat Perception: Anxiety often stems from a fear of the unknown or perceived threats. When these fears are not addressed or resolved, they can manifest as anger. For example, if a person feels anxious about their performance in school and perceives it as an unfair expectation, the anxiety can transform into anger towards teachers or the education system.

- Irritability and Frustration: Both anxiety and anger can lead to irritability and frustration. Anxiety may cause a person to become easily agitated or overwhelmed by minor stressors, while anger can amplify these feelings. When someone is anxious, their tolerance for frustration may decrease, making them more prone to anger.

2. Behavioral Manifestations

The interaction between anxiety and anger can influence behavior in several ways. Understanding these behavioral manifestations is key to addressing both emotions effectively.

- Avoidance and Aggression: Anxiety often leads to avoidance behaviors, where individuals try to escape situations that trigger their anxiety. For example, a person might avoid social gatherings due to social anxiety. On the other hand, anger can lead to aggressive behaviors, such as verbal outbursts or physical confrontations. When anxiety and anger coexist, avoidance behaviors may be replaced by outbursts of anger when the individual feels cornered or overwhelmed.

- Impulsive Actions: Both anxiety and anger can contribute to impulsive actions. Anxiety can lead to hasty decisions made in an attempt to alleviate stress, while anger can result in rash actions driven by frustration. For instance, someone who is anxious about a test may impulsively cancel study plans, while someone who is angry at a friend may react impulsively without considering the consequences.

- Conflicted Relationships: The interaction between anxiety and anger can strain relationships. Anxiety may cause individuals to withdraw or isolate themselves, while anger can lead to conflicts and misunderstandings. The combination of these emotions can create a cycle of relationship difficulties, where anxiety leads to avoidance and anger leads to confrontation.

3. Cognitive Processes

Cognitive processes play a significant role in how anxiety and anger interact. Understanding these cognitive mechanisms can provide insight into the emotional overlap between the two.

- Ruminative Thinking: Anxiety often involves ruminative thinking, where individuals repeatedly focus on their worries and fears. This cognitive pattern can contribute to anger when these fears are not addressed or resolved. For example, someone who is anxious about their future may repeatedly dwell on worst-case scenarios, leading to frustration and anger when things do not go as planned.

- Catastrophic Thinking: Both anxiety and anger can be fueled by catastrophic thinking, where individuals anticipate the worst possible outcomes. Anxiety may cause someone to imagine catastrophic scenarios related to their fears, while anger may arise from perceived injustices or failures. This pattern of thinking can exacerbate both emotions, making it challenging to manage them effectively.

- Blaming and Self-Criticism: Anxiety and anger can both involve self-blaming and self-criticism. Anxiety may lead individuals to doubt their abilities or feel inadequate, while anger may result in blaming others for perceived wrongs or injustices. This cognitive process can contribute to a cycle of negative emotions, where anxiety fuels self-doubt and anger leads to blaming others.

Recognizing Overlaps in Symptoms

1. Shared Physical Symptoms

Anxiety and anger can produce similar physical symptoms, making it important to recognize these overlaps to address them effectively.

- Increased Heart Rate: Both anxiety and anger can cause an increased heart rate, which is a common physical response to heightened emotional arousal. This symptom can be distressing and contribute to the overall experience of both emotions.

- Muscle Tension: Muscle tension is a shared symptom of both anxiety and anger. Individuals experiencing anxiety may feel tightness in their muscles, particularly in the neck, shoulders, and jaw. Similarly, anger can lead to muscle tension as the body prepares for a physical response to perceived threats.

- Sweating: Excessive sweating is another symptom that can occur with both anxiety and anger. The body's stress response system is activated in both cases, leading to increased perspiration and discomfort.

- Digestive Issues: Both anxiety and anger can affect the gastrointestinal system, leading to symptoms such as nausea, stomach cramps, or changes in appetite. This overlap in physical symptoms can contribute to overall discomfort and stress.

2. Emotional Symptoms

The emotional symptoms of anxiety and anger can also overlap, creating a complex emotional landscape.

- Irritability: Irritability is a common emotional symptom of both anxiety and anger. Individuals experiencing anxiety may become easily frustrated or agitated, while anger can lead to heightened irritability and frustration. The combination of these emotions can result in an overall sense of emotional instability.

- Frustration: Both anxiety and anger can lead to feelings of frustration. Anxiety may cause frustration due to the inability to control or predict outcomes, while anger may arise from perceived injustices or unmet expectations. Recognizing this overlap can help individuals address both emotions more effectively.

- Sense of Overwhelm: A sense of overwhelm can be a shared emotional experience for those dealing with anxiety and anger. Anxiety can create a feeling of being overwhelmed by worries and fears, while anger can lead to a sense of being overwhelmed by perceived injustices or frustrations.

3. Behavioral Symptoms

The behavioral symptoms of anxiety and anger can also intersect, influencing how individuals respond to various situations.

- Avoidance and Aggression: As mentioned earlier, anxiety may lead to avoidance behaviors, while anger can result in aggressive actions. The interaction between these behaviors can create a complex dynamic, where avoidance and aggression coexist or alternate in response to stressors.

- Impulsive Reactions: Both anxiety and anger can contribute to impulsive reactions. Anxiety may lead to hasty decisions or avoidance behaviors, while anger can result in rash actions or confrontations. Recognizing this overlap can help individuals manage their responses more effectively.

- Conflict with Others: The combination of anxiety and anger can lead to conflicts with others. Anxiety may cause individuals to withdraw or isolate themselves, while anger can result in confrontations or misunderstandings. This overlap in behavioral symptoms can strain relationships and contribute to ongoing emotional challenges.

STRATEGIES FOR MANAGING ANXIETY AND ANGER

1. Self-Awareness and Reflection

- Identify Triggers: Understanding the specific triggers for both anxiety and anger is crucial for effective management. Keeping a journal to track when and where these emotions arise can provide valuable insights into patterns and potential solutions.

- Reflect on Emotional Responses: Take time to reflect on your emotional responses to different situations. Recognizing how anxiety and anger interact can help you develop strategies for managing both emotions more effectively.

2. Emotional Regulation Techniques

- Practice Mindfulness: Mindfulness techniques can help you stay present and manage emotional responses. Techniques such as deep breathing, meditation, and grounding exercises can promote relaxation and reduce the intensity of both anxiety and anger.

- Use Relaxation Techniques: Incorporate relaxation techniques such as progressive muscle relaxation, guided imagery, or visualization to help manage physical symptoms associated with anxiety and anger.

3. Cognitive Restructuring

- Challenge Negative Thoughts: Cognitive Behavioral Therapy (CBT) techniques can help you identify and challenge negative thoughts associated with anxiety and anger. Reframing these thoughts can reduce their impact and promote a more balanced perspective.

- Develop Positive Self-Talk: Cultivate positive self-talk to counteract negative thoughts and beliefs. Affirmations and constructive self-talk can help shift your mindset and improve emotional regulation.

4. Effective Communication

- Express Feelings Constructively: Practice assertive communication to express your feelings in a respectful and constructive manner. Use "I" statements to convey how you feel and what you need, without resorting to aggression or blame.

- Seek Understanding: Engage in active listening and seek to understand others' perspectives. This can help address misunderstandings and reduce conflicts that may contribute to anxiety and anger.

5. Professional Support

- Consider Therapy: If anxiety and anger become overwhelming or unmanageable, consider seeking professional help. A mental health professional can provide tailored strategies and support for managing both emotions effectively.

- Join Support Groups: Joining support groups or participating in group therapy can provide additional resources and connections with others who are experiencing similar challenges.

6. Lifestyle Adjustments

- Prioritize Self-Care: Engage in self-care activities that promote overall well-being. This can include regular exercise, healthy eating, adequate sleep, and engaging in activities that bring joy and relaxation.

- Set Realistic Goals: Establish achievable goals for managing anxiety and anger. Break down larger goals into smaller, manageable steps to track progress and build confidence.

7. Build Resilience

- Develop Coping Skills: Build coping skills to manage stress

and emotional challenges. Techniques such as problem-solving, time management, and stress-reduction strategies can enhance resilience and improve emotional regulation.

- Foster Positive Relationships: Surround yourself with supportive and understanding individuals. Positive relationships can provide emotional support and help you navigate challenges more effectively.

THE CONNECTION BETWEEN anxiety and anger is complex and multifaceted, involving emotional, cognitive, and behavioral dimensions. Understanding how these emotions interact and recognizing their overlapping symptoms is essential for effective management and emotional well-being. By employing strategies for self-awareness, emotional regulation, cognitive restructuring, and seeking professional support, individuals can navigate the challenges of anxiety and anger more effectively. Remember, addressing both emotions with compassion and understanding can lead to improved emotional resilience and a more balanced approach to managing life's stressors.

CHAPTER 4

Identifying Your Triggers

Understanding and managing triggers is a pivotal step in addressing both anxiety and anger. Triggers are specific events, situations, or stimuli that provoke emotional responses such as anxiety or anger. By identifying and understanding your triggers, you can develop strategies to cope with and mitigate their effects. This chapter delves into recognizing personal triggers, keeping a trigger journal, and understanding the impact of triggers, providing detailed insights and real-life examples to help you navigate this complex emotional landscape.

RECOGNIZING PERSONAL TRIGGERS

1. Common Triggers at School

School can be a significant source of stress and emotional upheaval for many students. Identifying triggers within the school environment is crucial for managing anxiety and anger effectively. Here are some common school-related triggers:

- Academic Pressure: Many students experience anxiety and anger related to academic expectations. For example, Sarah, a high school sophomore, feels immense pressure to excel in her classes. Her anxiety peaks during exam periods, leading to feelings of frustration and anger when she struggles with difficult material. The pressure to maintain high grades can become overwhelming, triggering both anxiety and anger.

- Peer Relationships: Interactions with peers can also be a source of emotional triggers. David, a teenager, often feels anxious about fitting in and meeting social expectations. When he encounters conflicts with friends or experiences exclusion, his anxiety escalates into anger. This can manifest as irritability or outbursts in response to perceived slights or misunderstandings.

- Teacher Interactions: Student-teacher relationships can impact emotional well-being. Emily, a college freshman, experiences anxiety and anger when she feels that her professors are unfair or unapproachable. Discrepancies in grading or perceived lack of support can trigger feelings of frustration and resentment, affecting her overall academic experience.

- Extracurricular Activities: Balancing academic responsibilities with extracurricular activities can be challenging. For instance, Jake, a high school athlete, experiences anxiety about managing his time between sports, academics, and social life. When his performance in one area suffers, it triggers anger and stress, impacting his overall sense of well-being.

2. Common Triggers at Home

The home environment can also be a significant source of triggers for anxiety and anger. Identifying these triggers can help in developing strategies to address them:

- Family Conflicts: Family dynamics can be a major source of emotional triggers. Lisa, a teenager living with her divorced parents, often feels anxious and angry due to frequent arguments between her parents. The conflict and instability at home contribute to her emotional distress and impact her overall mood.

- Parental Expectations: Expectations from parents can also be triggering. Alex, a high school senior, faces anxiety about meeting his parents' high expectations for academic and extracurricular achievements. When he feels he is not living up to these expectations, it triggers feelings of frustration and anger, leading to conflicts with his parents.

- Household Responsibilities: Responsibilities and chores at home can be a source of stress. Maria, a high school student, feels anxious about balancing her academic workload with household chores. When her parents place additional demands on her time, she experiences anger and resentment, impacting her mood and overall well-being.

- Siblings: Sibling relationships can also be a source of triggers. For example, Kevin, a teenager with a younger sibling, experiences anxiety and anger when his sibling's behavior disrupts his personal space or study time. The constant interruptions and conflicts with his sibling contribute to his emotional stress and frustration.

KEEPING A TRIGGER JOURNAL

1. How to Track Your Triggers

Maintaining a trigger journal is an effective tool for identifying and managing triggers. Here's how you can start tracking your triggers:

- Choose a Format: Decide whether you want to keep a physical journal or use a digital app for tracking your triggers. Choose a format that you find convenient and accessible for regular use.

- Record Detailed Entries: When a triggering event occurs, make detailed entries in your journal. Include information such as the date, time, location, people involved, and a description of the event. For instance, if you had an argument with a friend at school, record the specifics of the argument, including what was said and how you felt.

- Note Your Emotional Response: Document your emotional response to each trigger. Describe how you felt (e.g., anxious, angry, frustrated) and the intensity of your emotions. This can help you understand the impact of different triggers on your emotional state.

- Include Physical Symptoms: Record any physical symptoms associated with your emotional responses. For example, if you felt a racing heart or muscle tension during a stressful situation, note these symptoms in your journal.

2. Analyzing Patterns and Trends

Once you have collected sufficient data in your trigger journal, analyze the patterns and trends to gain insights into your triggers:

- Identify Common Themes: Look for recurring themes or situations that consistently trigger your emotions. For example, if you frequently experience anxiety and anger during group projects at school, this may indicate a specific trigger related to group dynamics or workload.

- Assess Frequency and Intensity: Evaluate how often specific triggers occur and the intensity of your emotional responses. This can help you prioritize which triggers to address first and develop targeted strategies for managing them.

- Recognize Triggers and Responses: Analyze how different triggers affect your emotional responses. For instance, if you notice that conflicts with a particular friend consistently lead to heightened anger, you may need to explore ways to address the underlying issues in the relationship.

- Track Changes Over Time: Monitor any changes in your triggers and emotional responses over time. This can help you assess the effectiveness of your coping strategies and make necessary adjustments.

Understanding the Impact of Triggers

1. Short-Term Effects

Triggers can have immediate effects on your emotional and physical state. Understanding these short-term effects is crucial for managing your responses effectively:

- Emotional Reactions: Short-term effects of triggers can include immediate emotional reactions such as anxiety, anger, or frustration. For example, receiving a poor grade on an exam may lead to immediate feelings of disappointment and frustration.

- Behavioral Responses: Triggers can also influence your behavior in the short term. For instance, feeling overwhelmed by a heavy workload may lead to procrastination or avoidance of tasks, impacting your overall productivity.

- Physical Symptoms: Immediate physical symptoms may accompany emotional responses to triggers. These can include increased heart rate, sweating, or muscle tension. Recognizing these symptoms can help you implement coping strategies to address them effectively.

- Interpersonal Interactions: Short-term effects of triggers can impact your interactions with others. For example, experiencing anxiety about a social event may lead to avoidance or withdrawal, affecting your relationships and social interactions.

2. Long-Term Consequences

The long-term consequences of triggers can have a more significant impact on your overall well-being. Understanding these consequences can help you develop strategies to mitigate their effects:

- Chronic Stress: Prolonged exposure to triggers can lead to chronic stress, impacting both your mental and physical health. Chronic stress can contribute to conditions such as anxiety disorders, depression, and cardiovascular problems.

- Relationship Strain: Repeated triggers and unresolved emotional responses can strain relationships with family, friends, and peers. For example, ongoing conflicts with a sibling or friend can lead to persistent relationship difficulties and emotional distance.

- Academic and Career Impact: Long-term effects of triggers can also impact academic and career performance. Chronic anxiety or anger related to academic pressures can affect your concentration, motivation, and overall performance.

- Emotional Well-Being: Persistent triggers can contribute to ongoing emotional challenges, including mood swings, irritability, and decreased overall well-being. Addressing and managing these triggers is essential for maintaining emotional balance and resilience.

Real-Life Examples and Case Studies

1. Sarah's Academic Pressure

Sarah, a high school junior, experiences significant anxiety related to academic pressures. She is involved in multiple extracurricular activities and maintains high academic standards. During finals week, Sarah becomes overwhelmed by the volume of work and the pressure to perform well. Her anxiety triggers feelings of frustration and anger, particularly when she struggles with complex subjects.

To manage her triggers, Sarah starts keeping a trigger journal to track her academic stress and emotional responses. She identifies patterns, such as increased anxiety during late-night study sessions and feelings of anger when faced with challenging material. By analyzing her journal, Sarah realizes that setting more realistic study goals and taking regular breaks can help reduce her stress levels.

2. David's Peer Relationships

David, a teenager with social anxiety, often feels anxious about fitting in with his peers. He experiences heightened anxiety and anger when faced with social situations, such as group projects or social gatherings. His anxiety triggers frustration and irritability, particularly when he feels excluded or judged by others.

David keeps a trigger journal to document his social interactions and emotional responses. Through his journal, he identifies that his anxiety is often triggered by perceived rejection or exclusion from social groups. By recognizing these patterns, David starts working on assertive communication and seeks support from a school counselor to address his social anxiety.

3. Emily's Teacher Interactions

Emily, a college freshman, feels anxious and frustrated with her professors due to perceived unfair grading and lack of support. Her anxiety and anger manifest in feelings of resentment and decreased motivation. She struggles to communicate her concerns effectively and becomes increasingly isolated from her peers.

Emily begins tracking her emotional responses and interactions with her professors in a trigger journal. She identifies that her anxiety and anger are triggered by specific interactions, such as receiving low grades or experiencing a lack of feedback. Emily uses this insight to engage in open communication with her professors and seeks academic support to address her concerns.

4. Lisa's Family Conflicts

Lisa, a teenager living with her divorced parents, experiences significant anxiety and anger due to frequent family conflicts. The ongoing disputes between her parents create an unstable home environment, leading to heightened emotional distress.

Lisa keeps a trigger journal to document family conflicts and their impact on her emotional well

-being. She identifies that her anxiety and anger are triggered by specific events, such as heated arguments or changes in family routines. By recognizing these triggers, Lisa works on coping strategies, including family therapy and self-care practices, to manage her emotional responses and improve her overall well-being.

IDENTIFYING AND UNDERSTANDING triggers is a crucial step in managing anxiety and anger effectively. By recognizing personal triggers, keeping a trigger journal, and understanding the impact of these triggers, individuals can develop strategies to cope with and mitigate their emotional responses. Real-life examples and case studies illustrate how tracking triggers and analyzing patterns can lead to practical solutions and improved emotional well-being. As you navigate your journey to manage anxiety and anger, remember that self-awareness, reflection, and proactive strategies are key to achieving emotional balance and resilience.

Chapter 5

Practical Breathing Techniques

Breathing techniques are powerful tools for managing anxiety and anger, offering a way to calm the mind and body in moments of emotional distress. This chapter delves into practical breathing exercises, explaining their benefits, how to practice them, and how to integrate them into daily life. Real-life examples are included to illustrate how these techniques can be applied effectively.

1. Deep Breathing Exercises

Step-by-Step Guide

Deep breathing exercises are designed to engage the diaphragm fully, promoting relaxation and reducing stress. Here's a detailed guide to practicing deep breathing:

1. Find a Comfortable Position: Sit or lie down in a comfortable position. Ensure that your back is straight to allow your lungs to expand fully.

2. Place Your Hands: Rest one hand on your chest and the other on your abdomen. This will help you feel the movement of your breath.

3. Inhale Slowly: Breathe in slowly through your nose, allowing your abdomen to rise as you fill your lungs with air. Count to four as you inhale.

4. Hold Your Breath: Hold your breath for a count of four. This pause allows the oxygen to diffuse into your bloodstream.

5. Exhale Slowly: Breathe out slowly through your mouth, making a soft whooshing sound. Allow your abdomen to fall as you exhale. Count to six as you exhale.

6. Repeat: Continue this process for 5-10 minutes, focusing on the rhythm of your breath and the rise and fall of your abdomen.

Real-Life Example:

Consider Emily, a high school senior who struggles with test anxiety. Before a major exam, Emily finds herself feeling overwhelmed and panicked. She practices deep breathing exercises in her car before entering the exam room. By focusing on her breath, she calms her racing heart and clears her mind, allowing her to approach the test with a more composed attitude.

When to Use Deep Breathing

Deep breathing can be particularly useful in various situations:

- Before Stressful Events: Practice deep breathing before exams, presentations, or any situation that triggers anxiety. It helps center your mind and body, preparing you for the challenge.

- During Moments of Anger: If you feel anger rising, take a few minutes to engage in deep breathing. It can help you regain control and prevent outbursts.

- As a Daily Practice: Incorporate deep breathing into your daily routine, such as before bed or in the morning. This regular practice can improve your overall emotional resilience.

Real-Life Example:

John, a teenager who often gets into arguments with his siblings, starts using deep breathing techniques when he feels anger building up. By taking a moment to breathe deeply, he reduces the intensity of his anger and approaches conflicts with a calmer demeanor. This change in approach helps improve his interactions with his siblings.

2. Box Breathing

How to Practice Box Breathing

Box breathing, also known as four-square breathing, is a technique that involves inhaling, holding, exhaling, and pausing for equal counts. This method helps create a sense of balance and control. Here's how to practice box breathing:

1. Inhale: Breathe in slowly through your nose for a count of four. Imagine drawing a line up the side of a box.

2. Hold: Hold your breath for a count of four. Visualize the top line of the box.

3. Exhale: Breathe out slowly through your mouth for a count of four. Imagine drawing the bottom line of the box.

4. Pause: Pause for a count of four before inhaling again. Visualize completing the box.

5. Repeat: Continue this process for several minutes, focusing on the rhythmic pattern of your breath.

Real-Life Example:

Samantha, a college student experiencing anxiety about her future career, incorporates box breathing into her study sessions. Whenever she feels overwhelmed by her coursework or future uncertainties, she takes a few minutes to practice box breathing. This helps her regain focus and reduce feelings of anxiety, enabling her to approach her studies with a clearer mind.

Benefits for Anxiety and Anger

Box breathing offers several benefits for managing anxiety and anger:

- Reduces Stress: The structured pattern of box breathing helps activate the parasympathetic nervous system, which promotes relaxation and reduces stress levels.

- Improves Focus: By focusing on the rhythmic pattern of your breath, box breathing helps clear mental clutter and improves concentration.

- Enhances Emotional Regulation: Box breathing provides a simple but effective way to manage emotional responses, helping you stay calm and composed during stressful situations.

Real-Life Example:

Mike, a high school senior facing intense pressure from upcoming college applications, uses box breathing during moments of high stress. By practicing this technique regularly, he manages his anxiety more effectively and feels more grounded in his decision-making process.

3. Alternate Nostril Breathing

Instructions and Benefits

Alternate nostril breathing is a technique from yoga that involves breathing through one nostril at a time. This method helps balance the nervous system and calm the mind. Here's how to practice alternate nostril breathing:

1. Find a Comfortable Position: Sit comfortably with your back straight. Place your left hand on your lap and use your right hand for the breathing exercise.

2. Close Right Nostril: Use your right thumb to gently close your right nostril.

3. Inhale Through Left Nostril: Breathe in slowly and deeply through your left nostril. Count to four as you inhale.

4. Close Left Nostril: Use your right ring finger to close your left nostril, releasing your right nostril.

5. Exhale Through Right Nostril: Breathe out slowly through your right nostril. Count to four as you exhale.

6. Inhale Through Right Nostril: Breathe in through your right nostril. Count to four.

7. Close Right Nostril: Close your right nostril with your thumb.

8. Exhale Through Left Nostril: Breathe out through your left nostril. Count to four.

9. Repeat: Continue this pattern for several minutes, focusing on the rhythm of your breath.

Real-Life Example:

Sophia, a high school junior struggling with anxiety and sleep issues, integrates alternate nostril breathing into her evening routine. By practicing this technique before bed, she finds it easier to relax and fall asleep, resulting in improved overall well-being.

Integrating into Daily Routine

To incorporate alternate nostril breathing into your daily life:

- Start with Short Sessions: Begin with short practice sessions of 2-3 minutes and gradually increase the duration as you become more comfortable with the technique.

- Practice at Set Times: Choose specific times each day to practice, such as in the morning to start your day with a calm mindset or in the evening to unwind before bed.

- Combine with Other Practices: Integrate alternate nostril breathing with other relaxation techniques, such as mindfulness or progressive muscle relaxation, for enhanced benefits.

Real-Life Example:

Rachel, a teenager dealing with chronic stress from extracurricular activities and academic demands, adopts alternate nostril breathing as part of her daily self-care routine. She finds that incorporating this practice into her mornings helps her start the day with a sense of balance and calm, improving her overall resilience to stress.

Conclusion

Practical breathing techniques, including deep breathing, box breathing, and alternate nostril breathing, offer effective ways to manage anxiety and anger. By incorporating these techniques into your daily routine, you can enhance your emotional well-being and develop valuable tools for handling stress. Real-life examples demonstrate how these techniques can be applied in various situations, helping you achieve greater emotional balance and resilience.

Chapter 6

Mindfulness and Relaxation Practices

Mindfulness and relaxation practices are essential tools for managing anxiety and anger, providing techniques to calm the mind, reduce stress, and enhance overall well-being. This chapter explores mindfulness, guided imagery, and progressive muscle relaxation, offering detailed instructions and real-life examples to illustrate their practical application.

1. Introduction to Mindfulness

What Is Mindfulness?

Mindfulness is the practice of paying full attention to the present moment without judgment. It involves observing your thoughts, feelings, and bodily sensations with an open and accepting attitude. Mindfulness encourages a state of awareness and acceptance, helping you to navigate emotional challenges more effectively.

Real-Life Example:

Anna, a high school sophomore, finds herself frequently overwhelmed by her academic workload and social pressures. She starts practicing mindfulness to manage her stress and anxiety. By focusing on the present moment and observing her thoughts without judgment, Anna develops a greater sense of calm and control over her emotional responses.

Benefits for Teens

Mindfulness offers several benefits for teenagers, including:

- Reduced Stress: Mindfulness helps lower stress levels by promoting relaxation and reducing the impact of negative thoughts.

- Improved Emotional Regulation: By increasing awareness of your emotional state, mindfulness can enhance your ability to manage and respond to emotions more effectively.

- Enhanced Concentration: Mindfulness practices improve focus and attention, which can be beneficial for academic performance and overall cognitive function.

- Better Sleep: Regular mindfulness practice can improve sleep quality by reducing the mental clutter that often interferes with restful sleep.

Real-Life Example:

James, a teenager struggling with insomnia due to racing thoughts, incorporates mindfulness meditation into his bedtime routine. By practicing mindfulness regularly, James finds that he is able to calm his mind and improve his sleep quality, leading to increased energy and better overall well-being.

2. Guided Imagery Techniques

Visualization Exercises

Guided imagery involves using mental images to create a sense of calm and relaxation. Here are some visualization exercises to help manage anxiety and anger:

- Safe Place Visualization: Imagine a place where you feel completely safe and relaxed. This could be a real location or a place you create in your mind. Picture the details of this place

, such as its colors, sounds, and smells. Whenever you feel anxious or angry, mentally transport yourself to this safe place to find calm.

- Peaceful Scene Visualization: Visualize a serene and peaceful scene, such as a beach, forest, or meadow. Imagine yourself in this environment, focusing on the sensory details and feelings of tranquility it evokes. This exercise helps shift your focus from stressors to a calming mental image.

Real-Life Example:

Sophia, a college student experiencing high levels of anxiety about her upcoming exams, uses guided imagery techniques to manage her stress. By visualizing herself in a tranquil forest and focusing on the peaceful surroundings, she calms her nerves and improves her ability to concentrate during study sessions.

Using Imagery to Calm the Mind

Guided imagery can be particularly effective in calming the mind during moments of emotional distress:

- Before Stressful Events: Use guided imagery before exams, presentations, or social events to reduce anxiety and boost confidence.

- During Moments of Anger: When you feel anger rising, use guided imagery to transport yourself to a calming mental space, helping you regain composure and manage your emotional responses.

- As Part of a Daily Routine: Incorporate guided imagery into your daily routine to promote relaxation and enhance overall well-being. This practice can be especially beneficial during moments of high stress or when preparing for challenging situations.

Real-Life Example:

Liam, a high school athlete, experiences performance anxiety before games. He uses guided imagery to visualize a successful performance on the field, imagining the cheers of the crowd and the satisfaction of a well-played game. This mental rehearsal helps him approach his games with greater confidence and reduces his pre-game anxiety.

3. Progressive Muscle Relaxation

Step-by-Step Instructions

Progressive muscle relaxation (PMR) is a technique that involves tensing and then relaxing different muscle groups to promote overall relaxation. Here's how to practice PMR:

1. Find a Comfortable Position: Sit or lie down in a comfortable position with your body fully supported.

2. Start with Your Feet: Begin by tensing the muscles in your feet. Hold the tension for a count of five, then release and relax for a count of ten. Notice the difference between tension and relaxation.

3. Move Up the Body: Gradually move up through your body, tensing and relaxing each muscle group in turn. This includes your calves, thighs, abdomen, chest, hands, arms, shoulders, neck, and face.

4. Focus on the Sensations: As you tense and relax each muscle group, focus on the sensations and the feeling of relaxation that follows the release of tension.

5. Complete the Practice: Once you've worked through all muscle groups, spend a few minutes simply relaxing and enjoying the overall sense of calm

Real-Life Example:

Rachel, a teenager experiencing chronic muscle tension due to stress, incorporates progressive muscle relaxation into her evening routine. By practicing PMR regularly, she alleviates physical tension and experiences a deeper sense of relaxation, improving her overall well-being.

How It Helps Reduce Tension

Progressive muscle relaxation helps reduce tension by:

- Releasing Physical Tension: By tensing and relaxing muscles, PMR helps release built-up physical tension, leading to an overall sense of relaxation.

- Enhancing Mind-Body Connection: PMR increases awareness of physical sensations and the connection between mind and body, helping you recognize and address areas of tension.

- Promoting Calmness: The practice of PMR induces a state of calm and relaxation, reducing the impact of stress and anxiety on your body and mind.

Real-Life Example:

Mark, a teenager with frequent headaches related to stress, uses progressive muscle relaxation to manage his symptoms. By regularly practicing PMR, he reduces the frequency and intensity of his headaches and feels more relaxed overall.

Mindfulness and relaxation practices, including mindfulness meditation, guided imagery, and progressive muscle relaxation, provide valuable tools for managing anxiety and anger. By incorporating these techniques into your daily routine, you can enhance your emotional resilience, reduce stress, and improve overall well-being. Real-life examples illustrate how these practices can be effectively applied in various situations, offering practical solutions for navigating emotional challenges.

Chapter 7

Cognitive Behavioral Strategies

Cognitive Behavioral Therapy (CBT) is a widely used approach for managing anxiety and anger. It focuses on understanding and changing negative thought patterns and behaviors. This chapter explores the principles of CBT, techniques for identifying and challenging negative thoughts, and strategies for developing positive self-talk. Real-life examples are included to illustrate the practical application of these strategies.

1. Understanding Cognitive Behavioral Therapy (CBT)

WHAT IS CBT?

Cognitive Behavioral Therapy (CBT) is a structured, goal-oriented form of psychotherapy that aims to identify and change negative thought patterns and behaviors. It is based on the principle that our thoughts, feelings, and behaviors are interconnected, and that changing negative thought patterns can lead to improved emotional and behavioral outcomes.

Real-Life Example:

Laura, a teenager struggling with social anxiety, begins CBT to address her fears of social situations. Through therapy, she learns to recognize and challenge her negative beliefs about social interactions, such as believing that everyone is judging her. By changing these thought patterns, Laura gradually becomes more comfortable in social settings.

How CBT Can Help

CBT can help manage anxiety and anger by:

- Identifying Negative Thoughts: CBT helps individuals recognize and understand negative thought patterns that contribute to emotional distress.

- Challenging and Reframing Thoughts: By challenging irrational or unhelpful thoughts, individuals can reframe their thinking and develop more balanced perspectives.

- Changing Behaviors: CBT encourages individuals to adopt healthier behaviors and coping strategies, improving emotional regulation and overall well-being.

- Enhancing Problem-Solving Skills: CBT helps individuals develop effective problem-solving skills, enabling them to manage stressors and challenges more effectively.

REAL-LIFE EXAMPLE:

Ethan, a teenager experiencing anger management issues, starts CBT to address his emotional responses. Through therapy, he learns to identify triggers for his anger and develop coping strategies, such as taking a break and practicing deep breathing. This helps Ethan manage his anger more effectively and improve his relationships with others.

2. Identifying Negative Thoughts

Techniques for Spotting Negative Patterns

Identifying negative thoughts is a crucial step in CBT. Here are some techniques to help you spot negative thought patterns:

- Monitor Your Thoughts: Pay attention to your thoughts during stressful or emotional situations. Write them down in a journal to help identify recurring patterns.

- Look for Cognitive Distortions: Cognitive distortions are biased ways of thinking that contribute to negative emotions. Common distortions include all-or-nothing thinking, catastrophizing, and overgeneralization. Recognize these distortions in your thoughts to address them more effectively.

- Identify Triggers: Note the situations or events that trigger negative thoughts. Understanding these triggers can help you address the underlying issues contributing to your emotional distress.

Real-Life Example:

Olivia, a high school student experiencing test anxiety, keeps a thought journal to track her negative thoughts about exams. She identifies patterns of catastrophizing, such as fearing that a single poor grade will ruin her academic future. By recognizing these cognitive distortions, Olivia learns to challenge and reframe her thoughts, reducing her anxiety about exams.

Challenging and Reframing Thoughts

Once you've identified negative thoughts, it's important to challenge and reframe them. Here's how:

- Question the Evidence: Ask yourself whether there is evidence to support or refute your negative thoughts. For example, if you believe you'll fail a test, consider past successes and the effort you've put into studying.

- Consider Alternative Perspectives: Explore alternative ways of viewing the situation. For example, instead of thinking, "I'll never succeed," reframe it as, "I may face challenges, but I can learn and improve."

- Focus on Realistic Outcomes: Replace unrealistic or extreme thoughts with more balanced and realistic perspectives. For example, instead of thinking, "Everyone hates me," consider that some people may have different opinions or may not even notice you.

REAL-LIFE EXAMPLE:

Jake, a teenager struggling with self-esteem issues, learns to challenge his negative thoughts through CBT. He often thinks, "I'm not good enough," but by examining the evidence and considering alternative perspectives, Jake reframes his thoughts to, "I have strengths and areas for growth, and I'm working on improving myself."

3. Developing Positive Self-Talk

Crafting Affirmations

Positive self-talk involves using affirmations to counteract negative thoughts and promote a positive mindset. Here's how to craft effective affirmations:

- Be Specific and Positive: Create affirmations that are specific, positive, and present tense. For example, instead of saying, "I'm not anxious," use, "I am calm and confident in stressful situations."

- Use Personal Language: Frame affirmations in a way that feels personal and meaningful to you. For example, "I handle challenges with resilience and strength."

- Repeat Regularly: Practice affirmations regularly, such as during morning routines or before challenging situations, to reinforce positive thinking patterns.

Real-Life Example:

Natalie, a high school student dealing with performance anxiety, creates affirmations such as, "I am prepared and capable," to boost her confidence before exams and presentations. By repeating these affirmations regularly, Natalie enhances her self-belief and reduces her anxiety.

Using Affirmations in Daily Life

Incorporate affirmations into your daily routine by:

- Starting Your Day with Affirmations: Begin each day by repeating positive affirmations to set a positive tone for the day ahead.

- During Stressful Moments: Use affirmations to manage anxiety or anger during stressful situations. Remind yourself of your strengths and capabilities to stay grounded.

- Before Bed: End your day with affirmations to

reinforce a positive mindset and promote restful sleep.

Real-Life Example:

Lucas, a teenager dealing with social anxiety, practices affirmations such as, "I am confident and comfortable in social settings," before attending social events. This practice helps Lucas approach social situations with greater ease and confidence.

Cognitive Behavioral Therapy (CBT) offers valuable strategies for managing anxiety and anger, including identifying and challenging negative thoughts and developing positive self-talk. By applying these techniques, you can improve your emotional well-being and develop effective coping strategies. Real-life examples illustrate how CBT can be practically applied to address various challenges, helping you achieve greater emotional balance and resilience.

CHAPTER 8

Healthy Ways to Express Anger

Expressing anger in a healthy and constructive manner is crucial for managing emotional well-being and maintaining positive relationships. This chapter explores effective communication skills, physical outlets for anger, and creative expression as strategies for managing and expressing anger. Real-life examples are included to illustrate the practical application of these methods.

1. Effective Communication Skills

Expressing Feelings Without Conflict

Effective communication involves expressing your feelings in a way that minimizes conflict and promotes understanding. Here's how to communicate your anger constructively:

- Use "I" Statements: Express your feelings using "I" statements to take ownership of your emotions and avoid blaming others. For example, instead of saying, "You never listen to me," try, "I feel frustrated when I'm not heard."

- Be Specific and Direct: Clearly articulate the specific behavior or situation that is causing your anger. Avoid generalizations or vague statements. For example, say, "I am upset because you didn't return my call," rather than, "You never care about me."

- Stay Calm and Respectful: Maintain a calm and respectful tone when discussing your feelings. Avoid raising your voice or using aggressive language. Focus on finding a solution rather than escalating the conflict.

Real-Life Example:

Maria, a teenager who often feels frustrated with her group of friends, uses effective communication skills to address her concerns. Instead of confronting her friends with anger, she uses "I" statements to express how she feels and discusses specific behaviors that bother her. This approach leads to a productive conversation and improved understanding among her friends.

Active Listening Techniques

Active listening involves fully engaging with the speaker and demonstrating understanding. Here are some techniques for active listening:

- Give Full Attention: Focus on the speaker and avoid distractions, such as checking your phone or interrupting. Show that you are actively listening through eye contact and nodding.

- Reflect and Validate: Reflect on what the speaker has said and validate their feelings. For example, you might say, "I understand that you're feeling frustrated about the situation. It sounds like it's been really challenging for you."

- Ask Clarifying Questions: If you're unsure about something, ask clarifying questions to ensure you fully understand the speaker's perspective. For example, "Can you explain more about what you mean by that?"

Real-Life Example:

David, a teenager dealing with conflicts with his family, practices active listening during family discussions. By fully engaging with his family members and validating their feelings, David improves communication and fosters a more respectful and understanding atmosphere at home.

2. PHYSICAL OUTLETS for Anger

Benefits of Exercise

Physical exercise is an effective way to manage and release anger. Here's how exercise can help:

- Reduces Stress Hormones: Exercise helps lower levels of stress hormones, such as cortisol, and promotes the release of endorphins, which enhance mood and reduce feelings of anger.

- Provides a Healthy Outlet: Engaging in physical activity provides a productive way to channel and release pent-up anger and frustration.

- Improves Overall Well-Being: Regular exercise contributes to overall physical and mental well-being, helping you manage stress and emotions more effectively.

Activities to Try

- Cardio Exercises: Activities such as running, biking, or swimming provide an excellent way to release anger and improve mood.

- Strength Training: Weight lifting or resistance exercises can help channel physical energy and tension in a constructive manner.

- Team Sports: Participating in team sports, such as soccer or basketball, offers a social and physical outlet for managing anger and stress.

Real-Life Example:

Alex, a high school student experiencing frequent bouts of anger, starts running as a way to manage his emotions. By incorporating regular runs into his routine, Alex finds that his anger decreases and he feels more balanced and focused.

3. Creative Expression

Using Art, Writing, and Music

Creative expression offers a constructive way to channel and process emotions. Here's how different forms of creative expression can help:

- Art: Drawing, painting, or sculpting allows you to express and explore your emotions visually. Art can serve as a therapeutic outlet for processing anger and stress.

- Writing: Journaling, poetry, or storytelling provides a way to articulate and reflect on your feelings. Writing can help clarify your thoughts and emotions, making it easier to address underlying issues.

- Music: Playing an instrument, composing music, or listening to your favorite songs can help you express and manage emotions. Music provides a soothing and expressive outlet for handling anger.

Finding Your Creative Outlet

- Experiment with Different Mediums: Explore various forms of creative expression to find what resonates with you. Try drawing, writing, or playing music to see which medium helps you process your emotions most effectively.

- Set Aside Time for Creativity: Incorporate creative activities into your routine to regularly express and manage your emotions. Dedicate time each week to engage in your chosen form of creative expression.

Real-Life Example:

Emily, a teenager struggling with anger, discovers that painting provides a therapeutic outlet for her emotions. By regularly creating artwork, Emily finds that she is better able to process her anger and experiences a greater sense of emotional release and clarity.

Expressing anger in healthy and constructive ways is essential for emotional well-being and maintaining positive relationships. Effective communication skills, physical outlets for anger, and creative expression offer valuable strategies for managing and expressing anger. Real-life examples illustrate how these methods can be practically applied, helping you navigate emotional challenges and improve your overall well-being.

CHAPTER 9

Building Resilience Through Daily Routines

Building resilience is crucial for managing anxiety and anger effectively. Daily routines play a significant role in fostering resilience, providing a foundation for emotional stability and well-being. This chapter explores how to create a relaxation routine, manage time effectively, and develop healthy habits to build resilience. Real-life examples are included to illustrate the practical application of these strategies.

1. Creating a Relaxation Routine

Designing Your Routine

A well-structured relaxation routine helps reduce stress and promote emotional balance. Here's how to design an effective relaxation routine:

- Identify Relaxation Techniques: Choose relaxation techniques that work best for you, such as deep breathing, mindfulness, or progressive muscle relaxation.

- Schedule Regular Practice: Set aside dedicated time each day for relaxation practices. Consistency is key to building a routine that effectively supports emotional well-being.

- Create a Relaxing Environment: Designate a quiet and comfortable space for your relaxation practice. Use calming elements, such as soft lighting, soothing music, or comfortable seating, to enhance your relaxation experience.

REAL-LIFE EXAMPLE:

Sophia, a high school student struggling with stress, designs a relaxation routine that includes deep breathing exercises and mindfulness meditation. By incorporating these practices into her daily schedule, Sophia manages her stress more effectively and experiences a greater sense of calm and balance.

Incorporating Relaxation Techniques

To make the most of your relaxation routine:

- Combine Techniques: Integrate multiple relaxation techniques into your routine for a comprehensive approach. For example, start with deep breathing, followed by mindfulness meditation.

- Practice Before Bed: Incorporate relaxation techniques into your evening routine to promote restful sleep and reduce pre-sleep anxiety.

- Adapt to Your Needs: Adjust your relaxation routine as needed based on your emotional state and personal preferences. Experiment with different techniques to find what works best for you.

Real-Life Example:

Ethan, a teenager with difficulty managing stress, incorporates relaxation techniques into his evening routine. He finds that practicing deep breathing followed by mindfulness meditation helps him unwind before bed, leading to improved sleep quality and reduced anxiety.

2. Time Management Tips

Organizing Schoolwork and Responsibilities

Effective time management helps reduce stress and improve overall productivity. Here are some tips for organizing schoolwork and responsibilities:

- Create a Schedule: Develop a daily or weekly schedule to organize your tasks and commitments. Include time for studying, extracurricular activities, and personal time.

- Prioritize Tasks: Identify and prioritize your most important tasks. Use tools such as to-do lists or planners to keep track of deadlines and assignments.

- Break Tasks into Smaller Steps: Break larger tasks into smaller, manageable steps to make them less overwhelming. Focus on completing one step at a time to make progress.

Real-Life Example:

Maria, a high school student balancing multiple extracurricular activities and academic responsibilities, creates a weekly schedule to manage her time effectively. By prioritizing tasks and breaking them into smaller steps, Maria stays organized and reduces feelings of overwhelm.

Balancing Study and Leisure

Maintaining a balance between academic responsibilities and personal interests is essential for overall well-being. Here's how to achieve balance:

- Set Boundaries: Establish clear boundaries between study time and leisure activities. Avoid letting academic work encroach on your personal time.

- Incorporate Breaks: Schedule regular breaks during study sessions to rest and recharge. Use breaks to engage in leisure activities or relax.

- Pursue Hobbies: Allocate time for hobbies and activities that bring you joy and relaxation. Engaging in enjoyable activities helps reduce stress and promotes a balanced lifestyle.

Real-Life Example:

Jake, a teenager with a busy academic schedule, makes time for his favorite hobbies, such as playing guitar

and reading. By balancing his study time with leisure activities, Jake maintains a sense of fulfillment and reduces stress.

3. Developing Healthy Habits

Prioritizing Sleep, Nutrition, and Exercise

Healthy habits are crucial for building resilience and managing stress. Here's how to prioritize sleep, nutrition, and exercise:

- Get Adequate Sleep: Aim for 7-9 hours of quality sleep each night. Establish a consistent sleep schedule and create a relaxing bedtime routine to promote restful sleep.

- Eat a Balanced Diet: Maintain a balanced diet that includes a variety of nutrients. Focus on whole foods, such as fruits, vegetables, whole grains, and lean proteins.

- Engage in Regular Exercise: Incorporate regular physical activity into your routine. Aim for at least 30 minutes of exercise most days of the week to support overall well-being.

Real-Life Example:

Natalie, a high school student striving to improve her emotional resilience, prioritizes sleep, nutrition, and exercise. She establishes a regular sleep schedule, adopts a balanced diet, and engages in regular physical activity. By maintaining these healthy habits, Natalie enhances her overall well-being and resilience.

Maintaining a Positive Mindset

Developing a positive mindset is key to building resilience. Here's how to maintain a positive outlook:

- Practice Gratitude: Regularly reflect on things you are grateful for. Keeping a gratitude journal can help shift your focus to positive aspects of your life.

- Surround Yourself with Support: Build a supportive network of friends and family who uplift and encourage you. Seek social support during challenging times.

- Embrace Self-Compassion: Practice self-compassion by treating yourself with kindness and understanding. Recognize that setbacks are a normal part of growth and learning.

Real-Life Example:

Lucas, a teenager navigating academic and personal challenges, practices gratitude and self-compassion to maintain a positive mindset. By focusing on positive aspects of his life and surrounding himself with supportive individuals, Lucas builds resilience and manages stress more effectively.

Building resilience through daily routines involves creating a relaxation routine, managing time effectively, and developing healthy habits. By incorporating these strategies into your daily life, you can enhance your emotional well-being and resilience. Real-life examples illustrate how these practices can be applied, helping you navigate challenges and achieve greater emotional balance.

CHAPTER 10

Seeking Professional Help

Seeking professional help is an important step in managing anxiety and anger, especially when self-help strategies are insufficient. This chapter explores the benefits of therapy, different types of therapy available, and how to find a qualified mental health professional. Real-life examples are included to illustrate the practical aspects of seeking professional support.

1. The Benefits of Therapy

Understanding the Role of Therapy

Therapy provides a supportive environment for addressing emotional challenges and developing effective coping strategies. Here's how therapy can benefit you:

- Professional Guidance: Therapists offer expert guidance and support in navigating emotional difficulties. They can help you understand the underlying causes of anxiety and anger and provide tailored strategies for managing them.

- Safe Space for Expression: Therapy provides a confidential and non-judgmental space for expressing your thoughts and feelings. This safe environment can facilitate personal growth and emotional healing.

- Skill Development: Therapists can teach you valuable skills and techniques for managing anxiety and anger. These may include coping strategies, problem-solving skills, and communication techniques.

Real-Life Example:

Sarah, a teenager struggling with severe anxiety and anger issues, seeks therapy to address her challenges. Through therapy, Sarah gains insight into the root causes of her emotions and learns effective coping strategies. This professional support helps her manage her anxiety and anger more effectively and improve her overall well-being.

Types of Therapy

1. Cognitive Behavioral Therapy (CBT): CBT is a common and effective therapy for managing anxiety and anger. It focuses on identifying and changing negative thought patterns and behaviors. CBT helps individuals develop healthier coping strategies and problem-solving skills.

2. Dialectical Behavior Therapy (DBT): DBT is a form of therapy that combines cognitive-behavioral techniques with mindfulness and emotional regulation skills. It is particularly helpful for individuals with intense emotions and interpersonal difficulties.

3. Psychodynamic Therapy: Psychodynamic therapy explores unconscious processes and early life experiences that influence current behavior and emotions. It helps individuals gain insight into their emotional patterns and develop healthier ways of relating to others.

4. Acceptance and Commitment Therapy (ACT): ACT focuses on accepting negative thoughts and feelings while committing to actions aligned with personal values. It helps individuals develop psychological flexibility and resilience in the face of emotional challenges.

Real-Life Example:

Tom, a teenager experiencing difficulty with anger management, chooses to pursue Dialectical Behavior Therapy (DBT). Through DBT, Tom learns mindfulness and emotional regulation skills, which help him manage his anger more effectively and improve his relationships.

FINDING A QUALIFIED MENTAL HEALTH PROFESSIONAL

Steps to Finding the Right Therapist

Finding the right therapist involves several steps:

- Research and Referrals: Start by researching different types of therapists and asking for referrals from trusted sources, such as friends, family, or school counselors.

- Check Credentials: Verify the credentials and qualifications of potential therapists. Ensure they are licensed and have experience in treating anxiety and anger.

- Consider Compatibility: Choose a therapist with whom you feel comfortable and understood. A good therapeutic relationship is essential for effective treatment.

- Schedule a Consultation: Many therapists offer initial consultations to assess fit and discuss treatment options. Use this opportunity to ask questions and determine if the therapist is a good match for you.

REAL-LIFE EXAMPLE:

Emily, a teenager seeking therapy for anxiety, researches local therapists and asks for recommendations from her school counselor. She schedules consultations with a few therapists to find one with whom she feels comfortable and who has experience in treating anxiety. Emily's careful selection process ensures she receives the support she needs.

2. When to Seek Professional Help

RECOGNIZING THE NEED for Therapy

It's important to seek professional help when self-help strategies are insufficient or when you experience the following signs:

- Persistent and Intense Symptoms: If anxiety or anger symptoms are severe, persistent, or interfering with daily life, professional help may be necessary.

- Difficulty Managing Emotions: When you struggle to manage emotions despite trying various coping strategies, therapy can provide additional support and guidance.

- Impact on Relationships: If your emotions are negatively affecting your relationships or daily functioning, seeking therapy can help address these issues and improve communication and interpersonal skills.

Real-Life Example:

Mark, a teenager experiencing severe anger issues that impact his relationships with family and friends, recognizes the need for professional help. Despite trying various self-help techniques, Mark continues to struggle with managing his anger. He decides to seek therapy to address these challenges and improve his emotional well-being.

What to Expect in Therapy

Initial Sessions and Assessment

In your initial therapy sessions, you can expect:

- Assessment and Goal Setting: The therapist will assess your emotional challenges, discuss your goals for therapy, and develop a treatment plan tailored to your needs.

- Exploration of Issues: Therapy sessions will involve exploring your thoughts, feelings, and behaviors related to anxiety and anger. The therapist will help you gain insight into underlying issues and patterns.

- Skill Building: You will learn and practice various skills and techniques to manage anxiety and anger. This may include cognitive-behavioral strategies, relaxation techniques, or communication skills.

Ongoing Therapy and Progress

As therapy progresses, you can expect:

- Regular Check-Ins: The therapist will regularly assess your progress and adjust the treatment plan as needed. You will discuss successes, challenges, and areas for continued growth.

- Homework Assignments: You may be given homework assignments to practice skills and techniques outside of therapy sessions. These assignments help reinforce learning and facilitate progress.

- Continued Support: Therapy provides ongoing support and guidance as you work through emotional challenges and develop effective coping strategies.

Real-Life Example:

Olivia, a teenager beginning therapy for anxiety, undergoes an initial assessment to identify her goals and develop a treatment plan. As therapy progresses, she participates in regular check-ins and completes homework assignments to practice relaxation techniques and cognitive strategies. Olivia's continued engagement in therapy helps her make meaningful progress in managing her anxiety.

Seeking professional help is a valuable step in managing anxiety and anger, especially when self-help strategies are insufficient. Therapy offers expert guidance, a supportive environment, and valuable skills for addressing emotional challenges. By understanding the benefits of therapy, exploring different types of therapy, and finding a qualified mental health professional, you can access the support you need to improve your emotional well-being. Real-life examples illustrate how therapy can be effectively utilized to address various challenges and enhance overall resilience.

Chapter 11

Supporting Others in Managing Anxiety and Anger

Supporting friends, family members, or peers in managing anxiety and anger is an important aspect of fostering a supportive and empathetic environment. This chapter explores how to offer support, communicate effectively, and encourage self-help strategies and professional help. Real-life examples are included to illustrate practical ways to support others in their emotional journey.

1. Offering Support to Others

Empathic Listening and Validation

One of the most important ways to support someone struggling with anxiety or anger is through empathic listening and validation:

- Listen Actively: Give the person your full attention and listen without interrupting. Show that you are engaged through eye contact and non-verbal cues.

- Validate Their Feelings: Acknowledge and validate the person's emotions without dismissing or minimizing their experience. For example, you might say, "I can understand why you're feeling this way. It sounds really tough."

- Provide Reassurance: Offer reassurance and support by expressing your willingness to be there for them. Let them know that it's okay to seek help and that they are not alone.

Real-Life Example:

Emma, a teenager's friend, notices

that her friend, Lily, has been struggling with anxiety. Emma practices empathic listening by giving Lily her full attention and validating her feelings. By offering reassurance and support, Emma helps Lily feel understood and supported during a challenging time.

Encouraging Positive Coping Strategies

Encouraging the use of positive coping strategies can be helpful in supporting others:

- Share Coping Techniques: Suggest coping techniques that have worked for you or that you know can be effective, such as deep breathing exercises, mindfulness, or physical activity.

- Encourage Healthy Habits: Promote healthy habits, such as regular exercise, a balanced diet, and adequate sleep, which can contribute to emotional well-being.

- Be a Positive Role Model: Model positive coping strategies and healthy habits in your own life. Demonstrating resilience and effective coping can inspire others to adopt similar practices.

Real-Life Example:

Jake, a teenager supporting his sibling who struggles with anger, shares effective coping strategies he uses, such as physical exercise and journaling. By encouraging his sibling to adopt these techniques and modeling healthy habits, Jake provides valuable support and guidance.

---

2. COMMUNICATING EFFECTIVELY

Using Non-Judgmental Language

Effective communication involves using non-judgmental and supportive language:

- Avoid Blame: Use language that focuses on understanding rather than assigning blame. For example, instead of saying, "You always overreact," try, "I can see that you're feeling overwhelmed right now."

- Be Compassionate: Approach conversations with compassion and empathy. Express your concern and willingness to help without being critical or judgmental.

- Offer Solutions Gently: If you suggest solutions or strategies, do so gently and collaboratively. For example, you might say, "Have you thought about trying this technique? It might help you feel more at ease."

Real-Life Example:

Sophie, a teenager supporting her friend who is experiencing anger issues, communicates using non-judgmental language. By expressing concern and offering gentle suggestions, Sophie helps her friend feel supported and understood without feeling criticized.

ENCOURAGING PROFESSIONAL Help

Encouraging someone to seek professional help can be a crucial step in their journey to managing anxiety and anger:

- Normalize Therapy: Discuss therapy as a normal and beneficial option for managing emotional challenges. Reassure the person that seeking professional help is a positive step toward improving their well-being.

- Provide Resources: Offer information about local mental health resources and therapists. Help them research and find qualified professionals who can provide the support they need.

- Offer Assistance: Offer to assist with practical aspects, such as finding a therapist, scheduling appointments, or accompanying them to sessions if they feel comfortable with that.

Real-Life Example:

Michael, a teenager concerned about his friend's severe anxiety, encourages his friend to seek professional help. He provides information about local therapists and offers to help with the initial steps, such as making a phone call or finding resources. Michael's support helps his friend take the important step of seeking professional assistance.

3. Setting Boundaries and Self-Care

Maintaining Healthy Boundaries

Supporting others can be emotionally demanding, so it's important to set healthy boundaries:

- Recognize Your Limits: Acknowledge your own limits and understand that you cannot solve someone else's problems. It's okay to take a step back when needed.

- Set Clear Boundaries: Establish clear boundaries regarding the level of support you can offer. Communicate these boundaries respectfully to ensure that both you and the person you are supporting are aware of them.

- Prioritize Your Own Well-Being: Make sure to take care of your own emotional and physical well-being. Engage in self-care practices to maintain your own balance and resilience.

Real-Life Example:

Anna, a teenager supporting her friend through a difficult time, sets clear boundaries regarding the level of support she can offer. She communicates her limits respectfully and ensures she prioritizes her own well-being by engaging in self-care activities and seeking support when needed.

PRACTICING SELF-CARE

Practicing self-care is essential for maintaining your own emotional health while supporting others:

- Engage in Self-Care Activities: Incorporate activities that bring you joy and relaxation, such as hobbies, exercise, or spending time with loved ones.

- Seek Support: Don't hesitate to seek support from friends, family, or professionals if you need help managing the emotional demands of supporting others.

- Balance Support with Personal Time: Ensure that you balance your time between supporting others and taking time for yourself. Maintaining this balance helps prevent burnout and promotes overall well-being.

Real-Life Example:

Oliver, a teenager who frequently supports his friends, practices self-care by engaging in hobbies and spending time with family. He also seeks support from his own network when needed and maintains a balance between supporting others and taking care of himself.

Supporting others in managing anxiety and anger involves offering empathic listening, encouraging positive coping strategies, and communicating effectively. By encouraging professional help and setting healthy boundaries, you can provide meaningful support while maintaining your own well-being. Real-life examples illustrate how these strategies can be practically applied, fostering a supportive and empathetic environment for those facing emotional challenges.

CHAPTER 12

Overcoming Anxiety through Time Management

Anxiety is a shadow that creeps up on you, often when you're least prepared for it. It can feel like you're running a race against the clock with your hands tied behind your back. If you've ever felt overwhelmed by everything you need to do, paralyzed by the thought of where to start, know that you're not alone. Anxiety thrives in chaos, but you can starve it by taking back control of your time.

Understanding Anxiety: You're Not Alone

Anxiety is a complex emotion. It's not something you just snap out of. It tightens its grip when you feel out of control, but that's where time management comes in. When your day feels like it's running you, instead of you running it, anxiety digs in deeper. However, when you can manage your time well, you're telling anxiety, "You don't control me."

"Anxiety does not empty tomorrow of its sorrows, but only empties today of its strength," said Charles Spurgeon. This quote reminds us that worrying about tomorrow wastes the energy we could use today. Organizing your day can help you avoid this trap.

Breaking the Cycle: Time as Your Ally

Time management isn't about being busy. It's about being intentional with your hours. Anxiety often stems from the unknown: What if I forget something? What if I don't have enough time? The answer lies in planning. Imagine time as a puzzle — each piece (or task) has its place. It's easier to manage when you break it down, and suddenly, the overwhelm doesn't seem so big.

Start with something as simple as a daily to-do list. Not just any list though — be specific. Instead of writing "clean house," break it into parts: "Do laundry,"

"Sweep floors," "Wipe kitchen counters." These small tasks are more manageable and reward you with a sense of accomplishment each time you check one off.

Setting Boundaries with Time

Anxiety often comes from saying "yes" to too many things. Every time you say yes to something you don't want to do, you're saying no to yourself. Think about that. You need to set boundaries. When you manage your time well, you give yourself permission to say, "This is what I need to focus on today."

Eleanor Roosevelt once said, "No one can make you feel inferior without your consent." Apply this to your schedule. You have the power to prioritize your time, and in doing so, reduce the weight of your anxiety.

Actionable Steps to Combat Anxiety

1. Prioritize tasks: Focus on the most critical things first.

2. Use time blocks: Dedicate specific periods for specific tasks.

3. Rest is necessary: Don't feel guilty about taking time to recharge.

4. Evaluate your progress daily: You are doing better than you think.

You're in Control

You can't stop the waves, but you can learn to surf. Anxiety may never fully disappear, but with the right tools, it loses its power over you. By organizing your time, you reclaim your peace of mind. Give yourself credit — every step forward is a victory. You're not just surviving; you're taking back control.

CHAPTER 13

How Organization Can Soothe Your Anger and Anxiety

Imagine waking up in a cluttered room. The pile of clothes, the mess of papers — it's as if the chaos of the space feeds the chaos inside your head. When life feels disorganized, anger and anxiety have a way of sneaking in. But here's the thing: you have the power to take control. And by doing so, you'll feel lighter, calmer, and more in control.

Why Disorganization Fuels Negative Emotions

When your surroundings are cluttered, your mind often follows suit. There's a well-established link between external clutter and mental stress. Think about it — have you ever noticed how you feel more agitated in a messy room? Disorganization overwhelms your senses. It reminds you of everything you haven't done, and that can make your anxiety spiral.

Albert Einstein once said, "Out of clutter, find simplicity." Organization is not just about tidying your space — it's about clearing the clutter in your mind. A well-organized environment creates a sense of calm, giving your brain fewer things to stress about.

ANGER, ANXIETY, AND Chaos: The Perfect Storm

People often dismiss anger as a sign of weakness or a lack of control, but it's often a byproduct of anxiety. When you're overwhelmed and everything feels out of place, frustration bubbles over. Organization gives you something tangible to hold on to — it's a lifeline. When your external world is ordered, your internal world starts to follow.

Start Small, Build Momentum

Don't let the idea of getting organized overwhelm you. The process doesn't need to be perfect. Start small. Begin with your physical space. Clean a drawer, arrange your workspace, and suddenly, the knot in your chest loosens a little. Progress breeds progress. When you take control of one aspect of your life, it becomes easier to tackle the others.

The famous psychologist Jordan Peterson encourages people to "start by cleaning your room." It's a metaphor for managing the chaos of life by addressing what's directly in front of you.

Tangible Ways to Get Organized

1. Declutter your space: Pick a small area and clean it.

2. Make lists: Writing things down clears mental space.

3. Set up a routine: Create consistency to reduce anxiety.

4. Tidy as you go: Small, daily actions prevent things from piling up.

You Deserve Peace

You deserve to live in a space that feels good. When you create an organized environment, you're telling yourself that you're worth the effort. It's not about having everything perfect; it's about creating a space where you can breathe. You'll find that as your surroundings become more organized, your anger and anxiety will begin to soften.

Conclusion: Take One Step at a Time

Life will always have moments of chaos, but you don't have to live in it. Organization is a tool you can use to regain your sense of calm. It's not about making everything perfect — it's about making things better, one small step at a time. You've got this, and every step you take brings you closer to the peace you deserve.

CHAPTER 14

Mastering Your Time and Emotions

Emotions are powerful. When anger and anxiety take the wheel, they can drive you to places you don't want to go. But what if you could be the one behind the wheel? By mastering your time, you're also mastering your emotions. Time management isn't just about getting things done; it's about regaining control over how you feel.

#Time and Emotions: A Deep Connection

When you don't feel in control of your time, it's easy to spiral. Anger arises when you feel you're wasting precious minutes. Anxiety grips you when tasks pile up. But here's the truth: you're not powerless. By mastering time management, you're taking the first step toward emotional balance.

As Benjamin Franklin said, "You may delay, but time will not." Time is neutral. It's how you use it that matters. When you control your time, you control your life.

Turning Time Management into Self-Care

You might think time management is just about being productive, but it's much more. It's about protecting your mental health. Every time you say, "I'm going to schedule time for myself," you're setting boundaries that reduce stress. Time management is self-care in its truest form.

When you allocate time to yourself — whether for relaxation, hobbies, or just quiet reflection — you're telling yourself that you matter. Your emotions matter.

Practical Steps for Gaining Control

1. Use the 80/20 rule: Focus on the tasks that bring the most results.

2. Time block for emotions: Set time aside each day for self-reflection or a calming activity.

3. Avoid multitasking: It often leads to more stress and less productivity.

4. Practice mindfulness: Learn to be present with each task.

MANAGING EMOTIONS BY Managing Time

You're not just managing time; you're managing how you feel. By breaking your day into manageable chunks, you avoid the feeling of being overwhelmed. Each task completed is a victory — a reminder that you're in control. The small wins build momentum, easing the grip of anger and anxiety.

"Don't watch the clock; do what it does. Keep going," said Sam Levenson. This isn't just about pushing through — it's about understanding that you're always moving forward, even when things feel tough.

Conclusion: You Have the Power

Time is a resource you can use to gain control over your life and your emotions. Mastering time management allows you to dictate how you feel, not the other way around. Embrace your power. You deserve peace, and by organizing your time, you're well on your way to achieving it. Keep going — you're stronger than you think.

OTHER BOOKS FROM THE AUTHOR

DARLINGTON APPIAH

ALL BOOKS CAN BE PURCHASED ON AMAZON

MY JOURNAL FOR GIRLS

FAITH JOURNEY

A DEVOTIONAL JOURNAL FOR CHRISTIAN TEENS

A DEVOTIONAL JOURNAL FOR CHRISTIAN TEENS

Page

Don't miss out!

Visit the website below and you can sign up to receive emails whenever Darlington Appiah publishes a new book. There's no charge and no obligation.

https://books2read.com/r/B-A-NXJLC-IQOAF

BOOKS2READ

Connecting independent readers to independent writers.

Also by Darlington Appiah

Taming Anxiety And Anger